Copyright - David James

Thriving in the End Times - 2024

ISBN 978-1-0689652-0-3 - All Rights Reserved

PERMISSIONS:

(KJV)

Scripture quotations from The Authorized (King James) Version. Rights in the Authorized Version in the United Kingdom are vested in the Crown. Reproduced by permission of the Crown's patentee, Cambridge University Press

(NKJV)

Scripture taken from the New King James Version®.

Copyright © 1982 by Thomas Nelson. Used by permission. All rights reserved.

(AMPC)

Scripture taken from the Amplified Bible (AMPCE), Copyright © 1954, 1958, 1962, 1964, 1965, 1987 by The Lockman Foundation. Used by permission.

(TPT)

Scripture quotations marked TPT are from The Passion Translation®. Copyright © 2017, 2018, 2020 by Passion & Fire Ministries, Inc. Used by permission. All rights reserved. ThePassionTranslation.com.

TABLE OF CONTENTS

Chapter 1 – **Page 11** Who Am I? Why Am I Here? Where Am I Going?

Chapter 2 – **Page 36** Who You Are

Chapter 3 – **Page 50** Eternal Consequences

Chapter 4 – **Page 66** The Law of Sin and Death

Chapter 5 – **Page 83** Where Will You Spend Eternity?

Chapter 6 – **Page 103** Where Do I Go From Here?

Chapter 7 – **Page 118** Letting the Life of God Flow Through You

Chapter 8 – **Page 134** The Holy Spirit

Chapter 9 – **Page 147** The Holy Spirit and His Gifts

FOREWARD

Does God exist? Who is Jesus? Why should He matter to me? Where will I go when I die? We all have these burning questions in our hearts, now more than ever. As we try to navigate these unprecedented times, many are desperate for answers, but in this confusing age of limitless information - can they be simply and easily found?

Demonstrating a depth of insight into God's word, David James answers these questions in a no-nonsense, straightforward conversational style. A natural teacher, he translates the often complex and overwhelming concepts of the Bible into practical terms and makes them actionable. This easy-to-understand book can jumpstart your journey to start knowing and understanding what walking out life with Jesus is really like - right now.

It has been my pleasure to know David James as a member in our Warrior Notes Fellowship. Since joining us, I have watched him deepen in his relationship with Jesus to a place where the manifestations of God's blessing and favor are visibly active in his daily life. I have seen God supernaturally move on David's key obedience to saturate himself in His Word so He could bring forth an online ministry with his heart's desire to reach out and share the good news of Jesus. I have watched his life and family begin to transform powerfully through our prayers and his deep commitment to fulfill everything God has called him to. The contributions he brings daily through his online ministry and to each of us in our Warrior Notes Fellowship is a true testimony of what having a relationship with Jesus is really like.

Your Pathway to the Higher Levels, supplies the basic foundational teaching of how to come to know Jesus in a personal relationship, written in a simple and readable style. The reader's heart will be lifted and filled with hope and understanding that relieves their lost soul and hungry spirit longing to answer those critical questions and be lead into God's presence and love. I thank God for the blessing of knowing David James – though our time together has not been long, I see God's manifest presence in his life growing steadily and I can testify Jesus is indeed causing him to "Thrive in the End Times."

Jennifer LaChance –

Warrior Notes Fellowship Leader / July 2024

INTRODUCTION

Thank you for opening this very important book.

I have taken the time to write this for the person that has never met my friend Jesus before.

If you have no knowledge about anything to do with the Gospel, God, Jesus, the Bible or anything else surrounding it, I am confident this little volume will be informative, easy to read and most importantly, transformative.

If you have had exposure to church or the Gospel and have slipped or fell away for one or more varied reasons, this book is also made for you as I know it will fill in gaps and answer questions that you desperately need answers to.

I will take you through the truths that I have experienced as the most foundational, yet impactful elements that are absolute keys to a victorious life in Christ both now and into the next life.

What you are reading about here is not another religion. This is about a relationship with a PERSON who also happens to be YOUR GOD.

Our Father God and our Lord Jesus are God, but they are also "knowable Persons" like any others you will ever meet and get to know. and yet, God is not a HUMAN, but He is still a person with feelings, a will and emotions. It is from our Father God that we received our very human nature. We are literally His design, literally crafted by His hands and then breathed into with His own breath of the Spirit to give us life.

Jesus demonstrates the best of both being human and yet revealing the nature of His Father.

He was and is God but He was also a human man. This is what supremely qualifies Him as our Saviour in the first place, but His masterpiece of salvation was accomplished with all of US in the front of His heart and mind, so that we can make Heaven our home.

I hope that what is here inside this book, will move you forward in your life and in your eternity in ways that you can't even imagine yet.

I have walked with my Lord since 1980 and I can only testify, that after 44 years of relationship with my Lord, **He is worth it, but only because He thought you were worth it.**

Before I first came to the Lord, I was completely lost in my direction, confused about life and desperately lonely. I was one way, now I am another, and it is all because of My God.

Please use these lessons as a workbook. At the end of every chapter I have allowed a blank section for you to write down thoughts and questions as you are making your way through. Many of those questions will be answered further in the book, but I would encourage you, if they are not, to forward them to me by email so I can address them with new teaching materials.

I will see you on the other side…

Everything in this world has a value. In fact, the most practical way to tell what something is worth, is "what someone is willing to pay for it."

David James

Chapter 1 -

Who Am I...
Why am I here...
Where am I going?

Have you ever asked yourself those most important questions?

Have you ever, in any quiet or reflective moment asked, "what is it all about? Is there a God?

<u>What makes me – ME</u>, and how did that happen and whose idea was it?

The difference between the person who has asked that question and the person who has effectively answered that question is the difference between daylight and darkness or left and right...

You may believe that you are a "good person."

You may believe that you are at least as good as _____ who call themselves Christian, or "religious."

You may believe that there are many paths to God - "so why would I need this Jesus?"

*Jesus said to him, **"I am the way,** the truth, and the life. No one comes to the Father **except through Me.***
John 14:6 (NKJV)

That is the first, most important foundation we are laying toward complete faith in God.

Not long ago I was doing a contract renovation project in the home of a 90-year-old woman. She was still very lively and sharp which is obviously quite refreshing to see. Towards the end of my day there, as one question led to another, I told her about my ministry and that I was all-in for Jesus and His Kingdom and had been for most of my life. She really wanted my website address and YouTube channel information which I gave her on my ministry card. She desperately and sincerely wanted to know what I believed about God and Jesus and why it should matter that she should come to know Him at all.

My heart was both encouraged and broken by these questions, not because I didn't have the answers, but that I was sitting in front of an intelligent western woman who, for the most part, I painfully realized, had never heard the gospel.

My main ministry over 40 plus years of ministry has been to train and equip "believers for the work of the ministry," per Ephesians 4:11-12.

The Lord has since laid it on my heart to begin this comprehensive series of short messages for you who may have never heard the saving gospel of my Lord Jesus Christ or, if you have heard it, may have misunderstood it for one reason or another in different ways. These lessons were in part inspired by my encounter with this woman.

Teachers love "systems," and I am no different, so I will be systematically walking you through the foundations of our faith in this series of lessons so you will be able to easily use this information as a springboard for your faith in God through our Lord Jesus so you will hear face to face from our Master one day... "Well done, good and faithful servant."

We could all die and go to Heaven or Hell at any moment. There is nothing in the middle – between the two.

There is something called purgatory that was manufactured into the doctrine of the Catholic Church which was specifically designed to control the people so that more money could be extracted from parishioners. The idea, if you don't know, is that through "penance" and especially "payments" a family member can help a "questionable passed loved one" graduate from the "waiting room" of purgatory to Heaven itself or go broke trying.

This is patently false doctrine in so many ways I won't explain here, except to say that Jesus gives all kinds of second chances here on earth because you are still bound by this body of sin and need to receive Him, but when you are relieved of this body of flesh you will enter another realm.

It is ONLY what you do HERE concerning those most important eternal questions that matter at all toward eternity.

Two years ago, my own brother passed on at the young age of 63. This was a surreal encounter for me. He was my only sibling and everyone, parents, aunts and uncles have all moved on, to one place or another.

I have to admit that it really made me evaluate my own direction and calling before God. I pray nearly every day "Lord, help me not to miss it." I just want to please my God and hear "well done good and faithful servant."

Even though I've walked with the Lord since 1980 I am still always personally examining myself as Paul said, "whether I'm in the faith." I examine my heart regularly as David did saying:

Search me, O God, and know my heart; Try me, and know my anxieties; ***And see if there is any wicked way in me*** *and lead me in the way everlasting.*

Psalms 139:23-24 (NKJV).

I need to be sure that I am not walking in something else in my life that I am perhaps mistaking for faith in God.

Everything I teach on this, and any other subject is confirmed and will be confirmed with written scripture per the Holy Bible. Why does the Bible matter? Why are you using scripture to drive home every single point?

It is the Spirit who gives life; the flesh profits nothing. The words that I speak to you are spirit, and they are life.

John 6:63 (NKJV)

I don't just BELIEVE that the Bible is God's Word – I know it is. I have spent over 4 decades learning, through His Word and by the leading of His Spirit, how and what my God thinks about me and everything else.

We need to know that what is written, is for our benefit so we may begin to know and understand how and what our God really thinks about things that matter to us now and ultimately through eternity forward.

The Holy Bible is a 66-volume set, written over about 2000 years by some 40 different authors.

In western culture, it is unparalleled in the content and structure of its practical instruction for everyday living and conduct as well as wisdom for our daily lives and eternal future.

The Bible contains **some** of the "thoughts of God" expressed as Holy men of God were moved upon by the Holy Spirit. It obviously cannot contain all of who our God is, and what He is about, anymore than a backyard swimming pool can contain an ocean, but there is more than enough in the Holy Word of our God to know Him in a much deeper way than before we meet Him face to face.

The King James Version of the Bible (KJV) is far and away the best selling and most distributed literary work in the history of the world. There is nothing else anywhere in the world that is even close. I personally favour this one translation simply because it was my first Bible, and it is the translation I have taken the time to memorize more than any other.

There are a lot of Bible "versions." Some have made a diligent and deliberate effort to be word for word in their presentation, while others are more paraphrased. Please appreciate that our best Bible scholars through the century have done an amazing job at translating from the original tongues and manuscripts, but there will always be slight differences in emphasis and grammar.

Know that it is a fact, that you can still pick up, study and read any proper English Bible translation and lead a victorious and fruitful Christian life as you understand and follow it's commands and precepts.

So most common Christian "Bible versions" have value, but for those who can, the most important thing is to just simply start with one that you can read and understand.

The BEST Bible is the one you will consistently **OPEN** and **READ.**

Feel free to consider which is the best Bible translation for yourself when you become familiar with at least one of them.

I personally use my King James Version (KJV) a lot because I remember it, and it is an outstanding text that has stood the test of time. First published in 1611, it is, in my opinion, even from only a literary point of view, the greatest work of literature in the history of the world.

Even translations of the Bible that use words and phrases that are weaker in their grammar and translation value, still carry great power that you can use to live a victorious and fruitful Christian life.

Popular versions of complete Bibles I would personally recommend for reading or study are the King James Version, the New King James Version (NKJV), the New Living Translation (NLT), and the Amplified Classic (AMPC).

Be aware though, of the fact that your understanding will be much more limited outside of a true commitment of your salvation toward Christ than if you are just "fishing" through scripture to see if it makes sense.

Scripture rarely makes sense to an un-renewed mind so therefore the content of any writing is always skewed in one way or another by the person reading it.

The Word of God, His scriptures, in the end are "spiritually discerned." This means that natural understanding takes a backseat to spiritual understanding.

You will notice as you begin to read the Bible and spend more and more time in it, that every word and every verse is layered with a length, width, depth and height that is truly supernatural and an experience you can hardly describe.

Giving your heart and mind over to God the Father, through the Lord Jesus Christ is the only way you will ultimately have true understanding of WHO Jesus IS and knowing all that He did for YOU.

Unfortunately, the Bible, even among so-called "believers" is a book that is greatly revered in most church cultures but rarely read.

Whatever church body of believers that you end up connecting with, you must connect with one that encourages Bible reading and the practice of the study of the Word of God faithfully and consistently - or you are wasting your time there.

Through this entire study we are entering, please understand that your God actually wants to spend time with you to the point where He will "call you His Friend" because you have chosen to draw closer to Him. It has never been about filling up space and ticking attendance boxes each week.

Relationship with God, like any relationship, must be carefully and diligently nurtured and developed over the process of time and experience with that person.

His personality – God's very nature is clearly and consistently expressed and understood through the pages of scripture. This is another great reason why reading and meditating His Word is critical to your spiritual health in Christ.

God is calling you unto Himself.

He made you and values you more than you can possibly imagine.

The Bible says: 'GOD IS LOVE." At its core, which means that what is behind every thought He takes and every move He makes is His passion and desire over YOU and toward YOU…

For You formed my inward parts; You covered me in my mother's womb. I will praise You, for I am fearfully and wonderfully made; Marvelous are Your works, And that my soul knows very well. My frame was not hidden from You, When I was made in secret, And skillfully wrought in the lowest parts of the earth.

<u>Your eyes saw my substance, being yet unformed. And in Your book they all were written, The days fashioned for me, When as yet there were none of them.</u>
How precious also are Your thoughts to me, O God! How great is the sum of them! If I should count them, they would be more in number than the sand; When I awake, I am still with You.

Psalms 139:13-18 (NKJV)

If you have ever dated someone, perhaps someone you eventually married, didn't you think about them constantly BECAUSE you loved them and wanted to be with them, literally all of the time?! Our God is like that and so much more.

His thoughts towards me are more that the grains of sand. In case you were wondering, scientists estimate that there are 7.5 sextillion sand grains in the world. **That means that God has much more than a passing interest IN YOU!**

You, the created, were designed by an amazing creator for His pleasure and purpose, and I testify to you from over 40 years of direct experience with Him, that I always live to my highest and best purpose when it is His plan and purpose I am walking in. You have choices every day to go any direction you want for anything you desire.

But your loving God <u>asks that YOU DESIRE HIM.</u>

Have you ever purchased an item that needed assembly? You opened it up and you went ahead and started putting it together in the manner and way that appeared "obvious to you," only to discover, 2 hours later that those last pieces didn't fit, and "what's that thing for?" Then, you looked and discovered that the manual that the manufacturer included with the product had these pages in them with detailed diagrams and notes and numbers. There were even pages labelled in bold numbers, **1, 2, 3, 4...**

You are 20, 40, 60 or 80 years old now. You have watched how the pieces of your life never seemed to fit so much of the time. Things never seem to work too often. You and your family suffer through cycles of defeat and failure over and over, and you are sick of it.

Your God has provided an "owner's manual" for living as a saved and redeemed human person in a broken and fallen world called planet earth.

You have come to the right place so you can learn to put the pieces of your life together as He has designed you.

I say – you need JESUS. **You say** – for what?

I say – you need a Saviour right now. **You say** – a saviour from and for what?

I say – every person is lost in sin without Jesus. Jesus came to pay the price for your sin. **You say** – How am I responsible for anyone's sin and by whose definition am I in sin anyway and why does it matter?

Everything in this world has a value. In fact, the most practical way to tell what something is worth, is "what someone is willing to pay for it."

That someone in your life IS JESUS. He is man. He is God. He is your Saviour, and He paid everything on a cross of wood, but owned the hill on which it stood.

One day, all, great and small, rich and poor will either stand before their God in great trembling and horrible fear, doubt and self-loathing beyond description, or stand before their One and Only Saviour who gave everything so He might have you forever in His family eternally.

Nothing in this world matters until it does matter. But by then, if it's too late and you've left your body behind, all of this will mean everything – but it won't matter, because there is nothing you can do about the destiny you have confirmed either by your action toward God or your inaction…

This life has always been about YOUR choices. If you don't choose – another choice has already been made for you!

Every person will go the way of the grave someday. If you live to 150 years of age, the day is still coming, and you will give an account for what you did in and with this old body. You will stand before the one who made you and designed your perfect path before you were born.

As a believer there are great and eternal rewards for faithful obedience, and you will want to hear your Saviour say: "well done, good and faithful servant. Enter into the Joy of thy Lord."

The 90-year-old woman I met that day was as sweet and lovely as one can imagine, but she had no personal, working knowledge of her God and Saviour at all. Her one redeeming Godly quality at that point was that she was now asking the right questions…questions that have eternal value.

Just because you are reading this book, you have positioned yourself to not just hear the truth, but you are now able to ask the RIGHT questions.

So just what is SIN? At its most fundamental root - **Sin is disobedience to God.**

So, any person who knows what is right to do but does not do it, to him it is sin.

James 4:17 (AMPC)

Have you ever done or not done something that you felt wrong and conflicted about in your mind, heart or conscience. By whatever definition you used to describe it, "it just didn't FEEL RIGHT."

The voice of your spirit is actually the voice of God when it is properly yielded and submitted to God. You may never have been told by anyone that this or that was WRONG, but you just felt somehow that you'd be "missing it" to do or not do it.

God actually speaks to you and others all of the time and **you just were not aware it was Him.**

This process working through every person's conscience is the outworking of an inward grace that you were endowed with by your creator from the beginning. Though not complete, we have all witnessed a Godly nature as it tries it's best to break out through babies and children. We have all experienced the thrill that when we encounter the joyful laugh of a happy toddler. We really enjoy that because it is a beautiful reminder of joyful innocence.

Then, in a few years, the roots of sin grow up into the spirit and soul, and if they're not cut off early, those roots can grow into a wild bush that grows in any direction it wants, unless these Godly qualities of innocence and purity have not been ignored or even stomped on by those in our life that should have trained us.

But there really is hope - because no parent is perfect. Some are worse than others, but no matter how good or bad of a job they did with you, it was all to bring you to a moment like this, where truth is right in front of you – when your Father is speaking right to you.

Conscience confirms that even a person in the most primitive tribe in the most primitive setting in the world knows "it's wrong to kill and eat people." The truth of that is self-evident. It is because that very person will do all they can to not be killed and eaten by someone else. The apostle Paul said it this way:

*When Gentiles who have not the divine Law **do instinctively what the Law requires, they are a law to themselves,** since they do not have the Law.*

They show that the essential requirements of the Law are written in their hearts and are operating there, *with which their consciences (sense of right and wrong) also bear witness; and their [moral]decisions (their arguments of reason, their condemning or approving thoughts) will accuse or perhaps defend and excuse [them]*
Romans 2:14-15 (AMP)

I have met a lot of people in my life that obeyed their conscience fairly well and led "outwardly good and moral lives." But if they have heard the Gospel and "rejected it" - **these are in hell if they are dead.** The passage there in Romans 2 speaks to the potential redemption of someone who has NEVER HEARD and yet kept "the ESSENTIAL requirements" of God's Law – or not.

YOU ARE AN ETERNAL SPIRIT-BEING.

You are an eternal creature because you WERE made in God's Image and Likeness from the very beginning.

"Man"- IS A SPIRIT, he has a soul, and he lives in a body.

Now when I say MAN, I don't mean "male" or "female" any more than when I say giraffe or lion. There are male giraffes and female giraffes. If you wish to discuss anything else, you are in the wrong place. There are male-<u>men</u> and female-<u>men.</u>

Now, here is WHERE that conscience came from, that is: from where your personal, self-awareness came from:

*Then God said, **"Let Us make man in Our image, according to Our likeness; <u>let them have dominion</u>** over the fish of the sea, over the birds of the air, and over the cattle, over all the earth and over every creeping thing that creeps on the earth." So God created man in His own image; in the image of God He created him; male and female He created them. Then God blessed them, and God said to them, "Be fruitful and multiply; **<u>fill the earth and subdue it;</u>** have dominion over the fish of the sea, over the birds of the air, and over every living thing that moves on the earth."* Genesis 1:26-28 (NKJV)

In verse 26, **<u>God gave man DOMINION over EVERYTHING</u>** and man's desire and aptitude to be in control is God-given, but now, because of the "fall of man" through his disobedience to God, man's authority has been hijacked.

This is where the desire came from that every person has inside them - TO BE IN CHARGE. We begin to see this push for control starting in our 2-year-old children - it began right there in Genesis.

Ready or not, please declare by faith, this activation out loud with me right now before we move to the next lesson:

ACTIVATION:

Lord God, I can recognize that there is more going on in this world that I can right now understand. **Lord, I want to KNOW WHO YOU ARE, and I want to KNOW WHO I AM in relation to this world.**

God, I am asking You to open my heart and mind to see and know the TRUTH so I can be clear about who I am and what I am doing here in this world, and what my future holds.

THOUGHTS AND QUESTIONS:

_____

The default destination of every person on earth without Christ is hell and eternal damnation. So, just why does God send people to hell?

David James

Chapter 2 - WHO YOU ARE:

YOU ARE an eternal, spirit being.

You, as a human person - were made through wisdom and understanding by an eternal, intelligent designer Who designed you in His image and likeness as it pleased Him...

Things that have gone wrong physically or mentally in your life - are the direct consequence of and the direct byproduct of sin, unrighteousness and disobedience that have been passed down to every person through our spiritual bloodline.

The Bible FIRMLY TEACHES that every man, at his core is eternal, in God's Image and Likeness. As a result of that, every person ever born is accountable and responsible for the life that was given to him or her – by God.

You are answerable to your creator for who God made you to be and what you did with all of it. Let that sink in…

Every person who is still on this planet in their physical body is one breath away from eternal separation from that body.

The only thing preventing **the reality of "forever"** in your face is that body that has you fixed to this earth.

No matter how and what you currently believe about yourself, without a firm grasp of the eternal condition of man, this is a very high-risk position you now find yourself in.

The longer you put off the answers to the most important questions you will ever consider, the more difficult it usually gets to make the right choices when it matters the most.

Would you plan a 3-week European vacation with your family and not have some reasonable, if not ironclad certainty as to where you are going day to day, and how you will pay for it – and all the details in between!?

Obviously YES, and you would prepare for as many uncertainties as possible to minimize cost, discomfort and perhaps most importantly, wasting time. How much more certain should you be about where you are going when you one day leave your body? ...

You've seen friends, parents, and grandparents all eventually go by way of the grave year by year continually, do you think you have a magic easy button to somehow prevent all of that happening to you?

As a private contractor, I am in a lot of strangers' homes week to week and what I typically see are lives filled with just enough noise, visual stimulation and otherwise distraction to mask or avoid answering many of these most important questions. Typically, it's not unusual for TV's to be left turned on perpetually in these people homes, to a news network or some other work of fiction to which they attach themselves absentmindedly.

To NOT look yourself directly in the mirror and say "God, what about my future, and does it include you? – is pure, suicidal negligence on your part with lasting, eternal consequences.

Ignoring the outcome of your passing from this earth will not stop it from coming for all of us one day. Sooner or later, it will come for all of us.

*Jesus answered and said to him, **"Most assuredly, I say to you, unless one is born again, he cannot see the kingdom of God."** Nicodemus said to Him, "How can a man be born when he is old? Can he enter a second time into his mother's womb and be born?" Jesus answered, "Most assuredly, I say to you, unless one is born of water and the Spirit, he cannot enter the kingdom of God. That which is born of the flesh is flesh, and **that which is born of the Spirit is spirit.** Do not marvel that I said to you, **'You must be born again.'***
John 3:3-7 (NKJV)

So WHY DID JESUS **SAY** <u>we must we all</u> <u>be born again?</u>

When you were born into this planet of your natural parents, you carried all the physical, genetic traits of that family lineage, right? ...But you also carried something else from those parents that was not immediately apparent until later...

Have you noticed how behavioural characteristics get passed down through family lineage? How often we've seen children emulate their parents no matter how hard they may try not to:

Alcoholism

Promiscuity

Stubbornness

Lying

Stealing

Rejection

Fear

The actual curse of SIN is a lot like natural genetics in its transmission into a family bloodline. The actual curse of sin has been built into not just the genetic code of the physical man, but the curse of sin has been passed into the very spirit of every person ever born because of this original sin of disobedience.

The curse of **SIN had changed the very nature of man** from the very beginning.

*Therefore, as **sin came into the world through** **one man, and death as the result of sin**, so death spread to all men, [no one being able to stop it or to escape its power] because all men sinned.*

Romans 5:12 (AMPC)

This is the most fundamental reason why all men MUST BE BORN AGAIN. There is a spiritual DNA inside every person ever born that must be transformed and this is exactly what Christ came for...

Therefore, if anyone is in Christ, <u>he is a new creation;</u> old things have passed away; behold, all things have become new.

2 Cor 5:17 (NKJV)

To be born only once is to continue to live with, and in the judgement and subsequent penalty for sin that Jesus died and paid the price for. Hell is actually wasted on people. The Bible says that "hell was made for the devil and his angels," but the curse of sin puts mankind under a curse. This is a penalty incurred as a result of man's disobedience as he listened to the voice of his wife after she was deceived. All people everywhere will ignore this pending death sentence over their heads at their extreme peril.

The default destination of every person on earth without Christ is hell and eternal damnation. So, just <u>why does God send people to hell?</u>

<u>God never has SENT</u> anyone to hell. People's hearts and lives are so corrupted from the wicked elements of their sinful nature that their

spirit will literally "rush into hell on its own." Yes, the "final judgement belongs to God, but the actual verdict of "guilty" is a foregone conclusion without the redeeming power of the Blood of Jesus!

WHO desires *all men to be saved and to come to the knowledge of the truth.*

1 Timothy 2:4 (NKJV)

God cares about you and me because HE MADE EACH OF US, but for His Plan and Purpose, not your self-indulgence. This is The Passion Translation: this Bible translation is from the ancient Aramaic; a language Jesus and His disciples spoke to each other…

You formed my innermost being, shaping my delicate inside and my intricate outside,
and wove them all together in my mother's womb.
I thank you, God, for making me so mysteriously complex! Everything you do is marvellously breathtaking.

It simply amazes me to think about it!
How thoroughly you know me, Lord!
You even formed every bone in my body
when you created me in the secret place,
carefully, skillfully shaping me from nothing to something.
You saw who you created me to be before I became me!
Before I'd ever seen the light of day, the number of days you planned for me were already recorded in your book.
Psalms 139:13-16 (TPT)

God always has had perfect plans for you. He designed each person with His Purpose for you and in you – all based upon His design and intent, based on Divine wisdom, and understanding of all things.

The taint of sin in every man is the result of rebellion and it did begin in a garden. Don't try to picture the Garden of Eden as your favourite place with trees and shrubs in the city where you live. Instead, picture a place where there is uninterrupted fellowship, communion and communication between God, His Man and all of creation. Perfection was in all things, trees, dirt, animals, birds, and most importantly, His man.

You will discover as you read the account in Genesis, that it wasn't just the man that fell under the curse of sin, but all the earth and everything in and on it – because it was all under his authority, not God's...

This is the history of the heavens and the earth when they were created, *in the day that the LORD God made the earth and the heavens, before any plant of the field was in the earth and before any herb of the field had grown. For the LORD God had not caused it to rain on the earth, and there was no man to till the ground; but a mist went up from the earth and watered the whole face of the ground.*
And the LORD God formed man of the dust of the ground, and breathed into his nostrils the breath of life; and man became a living being.
The LORD God planted a garden eastward in Eden, and there He put the man whom

He had formed. And out of the ground the LORD God made every tree grow that is pleasant to the sight and good for food.

The tree of life was also in the midst of the garden, and the tree of the knowledge of good and evil.
Genesis 2:4-9 (NKJV)

This was life in the beginning. God brought all of the animals to Adam to name each of them. Adam and Eve walked and talked with God in this place because there was uninterrupted fellowship with Him, because they were obedient to it. His little family, Adam and Eve had uninterrupted, unhindered communion and fellowship with their Father God directly every day.

*Then the LORD God took the man and put him in the garden of Eden to tend and keep it. And the LORD God commanded the man saying **"Of every tree of the garden you may freely eat; but of the tree of the knowledge of good and evil you shall not eat for in the day that you eat of it***

you shall surely die."
Genesis 2:15-17 (NKJV)

Let me ask you a question: **Do you believe that you understand what death is,** any clearer than Adam and Eve did?

Please **ACTIVATE** this aloud with me right now...

My God, I ask you to open my eyes to the truth about Jesus. **I ask you to show me WHO I AM and WHO YOU ARE TO ME.**

I don't want to be lost. **If Jesus is my saviour, then I want Him and receive Him now.**

Forgive me for being stubbornly willful and disobedient to your plan for my life.

I repent of the darkness, disobedience and sin I have lived in, and I receive your forgiveness for all of it.

Jesus saves me now and I receive Him, Amen.

THOUGHTS AND QUESTIONS:

_____

*Then the serpent said to the woman, "**You will not surely die.** For God knows that in the day you eat of it your eyes will be opened, **and you will be like God,** knowing good and evil."*

Genesis 3:4-5 (NKJV)

Chapter 3 -
Eternal Consequences:

God created us all to not just be with Him, but to be like Him in every way, spirit, soul, and body...

Man was in fact so much like the One in whose image and likeness he was made from – that God made a separation, a distinction, which is; a boundary he was never to cross or there would be consequences.

Man was told that if he disobeyed, he would die. Do you think the man and his wife knew what DIE meant? - of course they didn't know.

For every person who was ever born - it is a common experience to "know what someone said" without fully appreciating the consequences for ignoring the command behind what was said to them. Your own child or grandchild may HEAR mommy or daddy say, "don't touch the top of that stove. It's hot and you will burn your hand."

Little Davey or Sarah will go on to appreciate and experience the full consequences of disobeying that through experience if they end up not obeying the word that was spoken to them as a warning first. The warning was right and clear, but that still does not erase the consequences of tender, pink child's flesh on a red element.

Does a small child KNOW what "hot means." No, but they soon experienced the consequences of "hot" a few seconds later. All mommy or daddy can do at that point, is place the fingers in some ice water or ointment along with a lot of kisses and hugs to stop the wailing.

The consequences for man were similar to the hot stove in how they started. God told them they would "die" if they did THAT, but they did it anyway. God forgave them, but it did not erase the consequences. All God could then do was use a "legal workaround" so that it all would not be a total loss.

Now after Adam sinned, they did not die physically, but something on the inside of them shifted, the light of God was extinguished and the separation of that sin and disobedience was upon them.

Now the third chapter of Genesis requires volumes of commentary to do it justice, but for our purposes let's satisfy ourselves with saying that this is where the change began in the man and his wife...

So when the woman saw that the tree was good for food, that it was pleasant to the eyes, and a tree desirable to make one wise, she took of its fruit and ate. She also gave to her husband with her, and he ate. **Then the eyes of both of them were opened,** *and they knew that they were naked; and they sewed fig leaves together and made themselves coverings.*
Genesis 3:6-7 (NKJV)

In other words, in verse 7 we see that this disobedience opened them up to something God did not want them to see, and He had already warned them severely about it.

God had literally walked and talked with man every day. What exactly was it that God was holding out on them about? I can tell you God held back nothing from his first family. He simply had set a boundary that could not be crossed, while at the same time could not be ignored because it was always present.

Please understand that we know "this evil one, the devil-satan had fallen in his own iniquity some time before that. We don't know when, but we do know that God told them to be on guard, nonetheless.

Do you suppose that in their daily conversations when Adam might have asked God a question about anything, that He would give Adam the hand and say, "I don't want to talk about it!" Of course not! Do good parents simply ignore their own children when they have questions?

Sin and darkness were what our God was preventing His man to look into – why? – because man was not equipped to look into darkness and survive the experience unscathed. This is why God had reserved and protected the knowledge of that tree for Himself alone.

So then, just what was it that God was shielding and warning His man about?

Now the serpent was more cunning than any beast of the field which the LORD God had made. And he said to the woman, "__Has__

***<u>God indeed said</u>,** 'You shall not eat of every tree of the garden'?"*

Genesis 3:1 (NKJV)

The serpent (<u>nahas</u>) itself was actually just another animal God and made but this animal yielded itself to the voice of sin itself as this creature was then in fact manipulated and used by satan himself to speak to and trick the woman. The scriptures teach that the woman was deceived, but the man himself willingly disobeyed. After the woman repeated God's commands that they were to leave this tree alone, this liar and thief then directly contradicted the Word of God concerning it...

*Then the serpent said to the woman, **"<u>You will not surely die.</u>** For God knows that in the day you eat of it your eyes will be opened, **<u>and you will be like God,</u>** knowing good and evil."*

Genesis 3:4-5 (NKJV)

Hold on a minute! Weren't they ALREADY LIKE GOD created in His Image and Likeness?

This evil entity, speaking directly speaking through the serpent said, "<u>you will not die</u>," – the direct, polar opposite of what God said.

***Then the eyes of both of them were opened,** and they knew that they were naked; and they sewed fig leaves together and made themselves coverings.*
And they heard the sound of the LORD God walking in the garden in the cool of the day, and Adam and his wife hid themselves from the presence of the LORD God among the trees of the garden.
Then the LORD God called to Adam and said to him, "Where are you?"
*So he said, "I heard Your voice in the garden, and **<u>I was afraid because I was naked; and I hid myself.</u>**"*
And He said, "Who told you that you were naked? Have you eaten from the tree of which I commanded you that you should not eat?"
Then the man said, "The woman whom You gave to be with me, she gave me of the tree, and I ate."

And the LORD God said to the woman, "What is this you have done?"
The woman said, "The serpent deceived me, and I ate."
Genesis 3:7-13 (NKJV)

In verse 10, **we see the first manifestation of FEAR** in God's man. This is always the first spiritual element that shows up in the nature of every person who is living without God on the inside. Every other misstep, failure and sin has its root in the manifestation of fear in it's most root form.

Here we even see the man actually accusing God regarding this - "woman YOU GAVE ME!" Unredeemed sin in a person's life always seeks to BLAME someone or something for the cause of their disobedience and failure.

I don't need to rehearse the thousands of years since then, highlighted by stealing, killing and destroying as a result of **this new seed of sin** that was now ever-present in the very genetics of the man's seed. This seed of sin, though the sperm

of the man into the womb of every woman was and is passed to every subsequent generation of

Adam though history until a person changes that lineage and becomes "born again."

Being "born again" was Jesus' COMMAND – not the invention of a preacher trying to talk you into one thing or another. Jesus said YOU MUST be born again because if you stayed just with the first birth it wouldn't be what God requires for you to be able to stand in His Presence.

The Bible says" Our God is a consuming fire." This is an important factor regarding the nature and substance of God. The Holy Fire of our God is part of His actual substance, but if your nature is darkness, sin and disobedience, you will never survive the encounter with your God.

He needs and desires you to be a functioning member of his family and household. In fact, you wouldn't make it over Heaven's threshold in an unsaved condition.

God left an enemy in the garden. This was man's test. Man was in fact was told by God to guard it. Don't forget what God told man:

*Then the LORD God took the man and put him in the garden of Eden to tend and **keep it.***

Genesis 2:15 (NKJV)

This word ***keep*** is interesting. This Hebrew word has all of the elements of watchful, diligent protection and means "to be on guard, circumspect and take heed."

A brief word about the "person of satan."

You'll notice that I don't capitalize satan as a proper name because it is not a name but a description. Satan means in the Greek: ***satanas*** accuser, one who opposes in purpose or act.

The character speaking through the serpent animal in the garden was this individual personified as "satan" - who in his original design was made by God as what is called a "cherub." This is a class or type of angelic being with a very specific purpose in their core. A "cherub" is not a fat, naked curly-headed baby with wings, but a throne guardian whose outstretched wings were designed to guard the glory of God Himself in His throne room.

Satan as a personality had a long history of rebellion against God of which we know some of the details but not all of them, obviously. One of the most descriptive passages on who this person is has come from the Prophet Isaiah. Much of chapter 14 discusses him in unusual ways. Here is the part I would like you to see…

"How you are fallen from heaven,
O Lucifer, son of the morning!
How you are cut down to the ground,
You who weakened the nations!
For you have said in your heart:
I will ascend into heaven,
I will exalt my throne above the stars of God;
I will also sit on the mount of the congregation
On the farthest sides of the north;
I will ascend above the heights of the clouds,
I will be like the Most High.'
Yet you shall be brought down to Sheol,
To the lowest depths of the Pit.
Isaiah 14:12-15 (NKJV)

The most important thing we notice is that he sought to exalt HIMSELF. Whenever you see PRIDE and self-promotion in any person, you can be sure satan is in it somewhere.

That word "Lucifer" is his name in the passage, but it is a very poor translation of the actual proper name that God gave him when he was created. This name and all the Godly Glory that came with it was subsequently stripped from him. This is the actual name that is in the text itself. This is the root word that the KJV writers translated **"Lucifer"** is actually the Hebrew word-name *"Helel"* meaning: shining one, morning star.

The complete history of the heavens and the earth are still mostly a mystery, but we do know from plenty of other scriptures what happened with *Helel/satan* and what his eternal future looks like.

The Bible says, "iniquity was found in Him." One of the reasons that there is no redemption for satan, is because he had no tempter to cause his fall, unlike God's Man who he tempted with sin to cause his fall. This made satan the illegitimate stepfather of all humankind moving forward. This might be the best reason Jesus said, **"You MUST BE born again!"**

"The devil made me do it!"

Flip Wilson, a man who was a popular comedian who had a TV variety show in the 1970's played a character named "Geraldine Jones." This was him in a wig and a dress - I'm not justifying the cross-dressing; I'm just revealing a prevailing attitude that still exists. She/he was well known for her saucy behaviour whenever she was called out for doing or saying something "naughty" - she/he would put hands on the hips and say: "the devil made me do it!"

How about you? Did the devil make YOU...do that...thing, whatever it is or was?

In some respects, satan is involved - **but it is the sin nature itself** - that is now present in the very core of the man on his inside, which is the real, eternal, severe problem that has to have an eternal remedy. You see, our Lord God is light and good and clean and pure in ways you and I cannot even imagine.

Sin simply cannot survive in God's Presence.

It isn't as if there is a back door to Heaven down a dark hall into a secret room where you and your sin can hide from your Lord and Creator.

You MUST come by way of the cross, by the Body and Blood of Jesus your Saviour in order for God to see you, receive you and accept you as a son in His House.

ACTIVATION:

Lord God, I ask that you examine me and "see if there is any wicked way in me and lead me in the way everlasting."

I repent of everything that is hindering me from walking in the fullness of relationship with You.

I will see you one day face-to-face, and I am determined to do it with joy because of what Jesus did for me and in me.

I submit to the death of the cross. I follow you and everything you said and did for me.

In Jesus' Name, Amen.

THOUGHTS AND QUESTIONS:

If God wanted to make "robots" that were programmed to always obey and never fail, that would be one thing, but our God wanted and needed us to CHOOSE HIM because we loved Him.

David James

Chapter 4 - The Law of Sin and Death

There are "laws of the spirit" that govern the world of the spirit you cannot see, just like there are laws of this natural world that govern our daily lives naturally. If there is a law standing against you for anything, there must be a higher law in order to supersede the consequences of the lower law...

There is therefore now no condemnation to those who are in Christ Jesus, who do not walk according to the flesh, but according to the Spirit. For the law of the Spirit of life in Christ Jesus has made me free from the law of sin and death.

Romans 8:1-2 (NKJV)

The Law of the Spirit of Life in Christ Jesus is the only law that an unredeemed person can turn to - in fact, if you haven't already, I would RUN to it. The law of sin and death will always be speaking against you and over you unless you invoke the higher law of Christ and His redemption over you. Understand what "redeem" means:

Redeem always means to "buy back." In a grocery store, as an incentive for you to buy a certain item, the manufacturer or store will buyback $1.00 on your pound of butter when the coupon is presented for this item at the checkout.

When you plead or declare "the Blood of Jesus" over your sin nature and disobedience, you are agreeing that your God, in Christ, now actually OWNS YOU – because He bought you.

When you are saying the words and agreeing to them, you are "agreeing to the transaction" Jesus made "in buying all of your sin – in order to give you His righteousness."

The consequences of the **law of sin** is that there is always death attached to it, and there is no escape from the lasting effect of that law outside of Jesus' Blood.

This law is immutable, unchangeable and irrevocable, but like many natural laws, it can be overridden by the implementation and activation of a higher law...Just like the law of gravity will keep a plane fixed to its runway until a higher law (the law of lift) is properly applied so it can go into the air, so in the same way death will always continue to work in a person **until he or she is "born-again."**

Death can and will only stop working in you and against you when you choose to die the death of the cross though your Lord Jesus. When a person is "born again" The Law of the Spirit of Life in Christ Jesus goes immediately to work to translate you from the kingdom or darkness into the Kingdom of God's Son.

The wages of sin: Sin pays, but you may not enjoy what it ends up buying. It always pays, but at what a horrible and lasting cost:

For the wages of sin is death, but the gift of God is eternal life in Christ Jesus our Lord.

Romans 6:23 (NKJV)

The free gift of God to redeem His man from the eternal condition of sin was accomplished by the gift of His own son "in the likeness of sinful flesh – condemned sin in the flesh."

In so many words, Jesus looked like us - but He wasn't entirely like us…To pay for the consequences of eternal damnation which the law of sin and death had set in motion:

Man's redeemer had to qualify to take our place as our substitute while legally standing apart from the taint of sin that was passed down upon us though the generations into the core of every man. The prophet Isaiah said this 500 years before His birth:

Therefore the Lord Himself will give you a sign: Behold, ***the virgin shall conceive and bear a Son,*** *and shall call His name*

Immanuel. Curds and honey He shall eat, ***that He may*** *__know to refuse the evil and choose the good.__*

Isaiah 7:14-15 (NKJV)

First, it looks like a contradiction. How does a virgin conceive a child if she's a virgin. Then we see something fascinatingly familiar in verse 15 that we first witnessed as a command of God in the garden: "... **that He may know to refuse the evil and choose the good.**"

The tree in the midst of the Garden was for God and God alone. This is the first clue we see about the identity of this Son as the coming redeemer. Sin was a test that only God as the Son could pass and never faulter or give in to it.

Only God Himself was eternally equipped to see the evil, know it's consequences, and yet NEVER choose it or succumb to its lies.

Now in the sixth month the angel Gabriel was sent by God to a city of Galilee named Nazareth, to a virgin betrothed to a man whose name was Joseph, of the house of David.

The virgin's name was Mary. And having come in, the angel said to her, "Rejoice, highly favored one, the Lord is with you; blessed are you among women!" But when she saw him, she was troubled at his saying, and considered what manner of greeting this was.

Then the angel said to her, "Do not be afraid, Mary, for you have found favor with God. And behold, you will conceive in your womb and bring forth a Son and shall call His name JESUS.

He will be great and will be called the Son of the Highest; and the Lord God will give Him the throne of His father David. And He will reign over the house of Jacob forever, and of His kingdom there will be no end."
Luke 1:26-33 (NKJV)

The Redeeming Son had to be a man to pay the price for fallen man while still remaining free from the sin nature that was passed down through the sperm of the man into every person.

Man carried the seed of sin and there was no stopping it unless God could bypass it entirely. To accomplish this, this redeemer had to be fully man while also being fully God, hmmm, sounds a lot like Adam before the fall, doesn't it? But this time the outcome is even much better and more far reaching in it's purpose and destiny than even Adam was before his fall. In fact, Jesus is called in scripture "the last Adam" – with the obvious difference, when He came, He chose the right and got it right. This is what qualified Jesus to be our Saviour, but the completed work between His birth and final ascension still had to be done in every minute, prophetic detail > flawlessly, and it was.

Therefore, if anyone is in Christ, **he is a new creation;** *old things have passed away; behold, all things have become new.*

Whatever and whoever you were before you made Jesus your Lord, Saviour and Redeemer, by choosing HIM, has literally made you a new species that is still an individual and yet only fully complete in Christ BECAUSE OF YOUR FAITH IN HIM and all that He did for you.

Now all things are of God, who has reconciled us to Himself through Jesus Christ, and has given us the ministry of reconciliation, that is, that God was in Christ reconciling the world to Himself, not imputing their trespasses to them, and has committed to us the word of reconciliation.

Now then, we are ambassadors for Christ, as though God were pleading through us: **we implore you on Christ's behalf, be reconciled to God.**

<u>For He made Him who knew no sin to be sin for us, that we might become the righteousness of God in Him.</u>

2 Cor. 5:17-21 (NKJV)

It was what God allowed to happen and what His Son Jesus submitted to between His arrest and His ascension that finally positioned each of us so that we could be MADE LIKE HIM.

In other words, Jesus was "MADE SIN" so you could be "MADE RIGHTEOUS."

You and I HAD TO BE MADE righteous in the eyes of our Father God so that He would never in fact SEE OUR SIN. Jesus had to be MADE SIN because of our disobedience so He could buy us back, and He was the only one that could survive the encounter of taking upon Himself, the sin of the entire world.

The results were so far reaching, all inclusive and complete that **it is literally as if the believer had NEVER SINNED** in the eyes of God.

*For I will be merciful to their unrighteousness, and **their sins and their iniquities will I remember no more.***

Hebrews 8:12 (KJV)

It's quite mind boggling to consider that our God's masterpiece of redemption was so far reaching that it's literally as if YOU have never failed at anything EVER and **God and Heaven has no memory or record of it**. Before Jesus ever went to the cross, David the Psalmist/King prophesied…

*For as the heavens are high above the earth, so **great is His mercy** toward those who fear Him.*

*As far as the east is from the west, **so far has He removed our transgressions from us.***

Psalms 103:11-12 (NKJV)

Faith in Christ gives each of us position and standing to come back to our Father, where we first started and where we all began and truly belong. It is not God's fault if any person does not receive the price paid for sin.

God has made every provision for your redemption. God's effort to buy you back from the brink goes back to even to before you were created...

*Then the King will say to those on His right hand, 'Come, you blessed of My Father, inherit the kingdom prepared for you from the **foundation** of the world:*

Matthew 25:34 (NKJV)

That word **foundation means "conception."** Before you were you, God thought of you, designed you to be IN CHRIST from the beginning. Even before the first man was actually born, the knowledge of the divine plan was that the man would fall, and therefore, redemption was built into the plan as God's masterpiece of man's complete redemption that would be altogether irrevocable and irrefutable. Nothing like a serpent in the garden would ever be able to trick you or talk you out of what God had set in motion.

If God wanted to make "robots" that were programmed to always obey and never fail, that would be one thing, **but our God wanted**

and needed us to CHOOSE HIM because we loved Him.

This is how God would get a family that would learn to "choose the good" in spite of the temptation to sin. This successful completion of this scenario can only be done though faith in Jesus.

Our God has made it clear that He wants a family. How would it go down in the long term if your children were MADE to love and serve you? Is that true love or service from a pure heart? - It can't be.

Our God IS LOVE. He is also light in whom no darkness can dwell or come near.

We all need to come to God by THE WAY and design that God has put in place, for there is no other way or provision for that access:

*let it be known to you all, and to all the people of Israel, that **by the name of Jesus***

Christ of Nazareth, *whom you crucified, whom God raised from the dead, by Him this man stands here before you whole.*

This is the 'stone which was rejected by you builders, which has become the chief cornerstone.'

Nor is there salvation in any other, ***for there is no other name under heaven given among men by which we must be saved.***"

Acts 4:10-12 (NKJV)

God did not designate Buddha or Krishna or Shiva or Joseph Smith, the Pope, or even your pastor or any other minister to become or act as stand-in for you to come and stand before God for you or with you. These failed "prophets" are dead and moldering in the ground. Our redeeming Saviour is seated at His Father's right hand now and He asks you to be with Him where He is.

Every person will stand before God and give an account for what each has done with what was required of them and written about them.

Only Jesus, His Body and His Blood was sufficient to pay the price to buy back His man from his sin and darkness:

"Let not your heart be troubled; you believe in God, believe also in Me. In My Father's house are many mansions; if it were not so, I would have told you. I go to prepare a place for you. And if I go and prepare a place for you, I will come again and receive you to Myself; that where I am, there you may be also. And where I go you know, and the way you know."

Thomas said to Him, "Lord, we do not know where You are going, and how can we know the way?"

Jesus said to him, **_"I am the way, the truth, and the life. No one comes to the Father except through Me._**

John 14:1-6 (NKJV)

WHO IS THE WAY? **Only Jesus is the way. Anything else you may try is not His Way,** stop it right now and receive Jesus. It is not Jesus **"<u>and</u>"** – <u>it is ONLY Jesus and no one beside Him.</u>

ACTIVATION:

Please pray with me aloud as I read this:

My Father God, I receive Jesus and what He did as the consequence for my disobedience and sin.

Jesus died for me so I can live for Him.

Father, I ask you to show me the truth about what you have done, everyday as I commit and submit to You and Your Word, in Jesus' Name, Amen.

THOUGHTS AND QUESTIONS:

_____

If a person doesn't want anything to do with God, there is an eternal place reserved for those where there is nothing to do with God.

Bill Weise

Chapter 5 - Where will you spend Eternity?

The entire mosaic of the Word of God teaches throughout, that every man will, spend their eternal existence in one of two places: in hell, separated from God or united with Him forever in Heaven. The thing that makes hell – HELL more than anything else is that there is NOTHING TO DO WITH GOD THERE.

That is simply how many people want to have it - and they will get what they wanted, until they realize how much of the goodness of God they had not acknowledged and had taken for granted in a life that had been lived carelessly and frivolously.

Blessed be the God and Father of our Lord Jesus Christ, who according to His abundant mercy has begotten us again to a living hope through the resurrection of Jesus Christ from the dead, **_to an inheritance incorruptible and undefiled and that does not fade away, reserved in heaven for you,_**

who are kept by the power of God

through faith for salvation ready to be revealed in the last time.

1 Peter 1:3-5 (KJV)

"Reserved in Heaven for you" Are you prepared to see your reservation cancelled or go unused?

The next scripture indicates God's intent as every man at one point had their name in God's Book of Life, but that it is possible that Jesus will blot out a person's name from that book... Adam and Eve upon their sin in the Garden, but then, if man is a spirit-being in his true nature, what does eternal, spiritual separation look like?

The Son of man shall send forth his angels, and they shall gather out of his kingdom all things that offend, and them which do iniquity; And shall cast them into a furnace of fire: there shall be wailing and gnashing of teeth.

Then shall the righteous shine forth as the sun in the kingdom of their Father. Who hath ears to hear, let him hear.

Matthew 13:41-43 (KJV)

And I saw a great white throne, and him that sat on it, from whose face the earth and the heaven fled away; and there was found no place for them.

<u>***And I saw the dead, small and great, stand before God; and the books were opened: and another book was opened, which is the book of life:***</u> *and the dead were judged out of those things which were written in the books, according to their works.*

And the sea gave up the dead which were in it; and death and hell delivered up the dead which were in them: and they were judged every man according to their works.

And death and hell were cast into the lake of fire. This is the second death. ***And***

whosoever was not found written in the book of life was cast into the lake of fire.

Revelation 20:11-15 (KJV)

Verse 15 above, says that if your name is not "written in the Book of Life" you will be eternally damned and lost to an eternity without Him.

What is the BOOK OF LIFE?

This is Heaven's official register of all of those who had and will have chosen God's path and Way of salvation. Only our God carries this foreknowledge, but the choice is still yours to make and always will be. There is no other name anywhere or in any place or time by which you can be saved because Jesus was one sacrifice for all - for all of time.

Before Jesus came in person 2000 years ago there were many righteous saints of the Old Testament before He went to the cross who were saved looking forward and ahead to Jesus' death and resurrection, just as there is now many multiplied millions of true, **Christian believers, who are saved looking back at what He did** so they can walk in that new life He gives right here and now.

Jesus' life and salvation is not an end in itself for the believer, but a new life and purpose that is given purposely and deliberately to God every day as each "believing one" walks and lives in ways that are in obedience to what our God has asked of each one of us.

Every person ever born will be judged in some way or form, but every believer <u>in Christ</u> will be judged by his deeds and actions IN CHRIST because of His faith in Christ. This is called the judgement seat of Christ. This is a determination of rewards for obedience to His Name and His Calling as believers, not to determine if God will let you into Heaven.

Every believer who is at this judgment is entering Heaven. When you are judged for rewards, it means you will never be judged for your sins.

There is another final judgment for all unbelievers who find themselves outside of Christ's Blood and redemption. In this judgement, each person will personally have to stand up for what each has done on their own merits – without Christ as their Lord or in their life. Unfortunately for these people, they will stand before the judge of the universe on their own merits without Christ. This is the ticket to hell that their life outside of Christ has bargained for and the results are unchangeable.

Anything you do or say outside of Christ is never perfect enough to pay for what and who sin has made you. This is why we need Jesus to stand between us and the sin that testifies against us and make it bow to His Name when you confessed Him as Lord and Saviour. What Jesus paid for with His broken Body and Blood is so complete that Paul the apostle boldly declares:

For we have not a high priest which cannot be touched with the feeling of our infirmities; but was in all points tempted like as we are, yet without sin. Let us therefore come boldly unto the throne of grace, that we may obtain mercy, and find grace to help in time of need.

Hebrews 4:15-16 (KJV)

Jesus gloriously passed every test that we failed so that we would not just be accepted by joyfully welcomed before the very Face of our Living God! There is one eternal standard that our God always has and always will live by: PERFECTION and only Jesus lived up to that.

Levels of torment and judgment are determined by what people did or did not do concerning accepting Christ's free gift of righteousness, as opposed to levels of blessing and eternal reward for those who walked out their faith in Christ upon the earth while they had the chance.

Many ask - "would or should a "loving God" allow someone to be tormented for their sin and unbelief forever - **does that seem right or fair?**

Ask this instead: Would a "loving God" try to force or manipulate a person into an unwilling decision to have fellowship, friendship or an eternal place with Himself, **against their personal desires,** wishes or overall inclinations - **just because God chooses it** for them - and not the person? Is that remotely right or fair?

If you wanted to move from where you live now, to the city of Seattle Washington, and arrived in town with your truck and trailer at the home that is on the top of the highest hill, a house that is at least 20.000 square feet, with a lap pool, a six-car garage and servants - then pounded on the door and demanded –

*"Let me in to stay at your place for the next 10 years, in fact I think I'll just permanently retire here. You have plenty of room in your mansion, and after all, **I'm a good person!**"*

What would and should this person say to you?

"Dude, I don't know you, get you and your stuff off of my property in the next 30 seconds or I am calling the police, or I might just take matters into my own hands."

Jesus told a parable about this type of situation:

Then the king said to the servants, 'Bind him hand and foot, take him away, and cast him into outer darkness; there will be weeping and gnashing of teeth.' For many are called, but few are chosen."
Matthew 22:13-14 (NKJV)

The simplest answer as to WHY GOD cannot and will not accept everyone in His House is because **there is no established RELATIONSHIP or FELLOWSHIP.**

Would you necessarily ACCEPT just anyone into your own home without any foreknowledge of them or even personal relationship. Would you let a stranger of any kind into your house where your children sleep? Obviously not, unless you are stupid or insane…

It is BECAUSE you have the choice of free will that you MUST CHOOSE, and <u>if you</u> don't **<u>choose wisely, a choice has already been made for you.</u>**

There are clear and consistent warnings that you need to act upon NOW.

Who wishes all men to be saved and [increasingly] to perceive and recognize and discern and know precisely and correctly

the [divine] Truth.

For there [is only] one God, and [only] one Mediator between God and men, the Man Christ Jesus,
Who gave Himself as a ransom for all [people, a fact that was] attested to at the right and proper time.

1 Timothy 2:4-6 (AMPC)

God desires YOU, but do you desire HIM? Do you MAKE your children love you? If they drift away from your love and embrace, do you "actually STOP LOVING THEM?"

If you don't have grown children of your own, you may not appreciate the heartache a good parent goes though when they are estranged from a child. You don't stop loving them no matter what, but that doesn't change the fact that they will still make their own choices and suffer the dire consequences. So, how would you like to be held to account for everything outside of Christ – in judgment and punishment eternally for your crimes?! This is the eternal end and consequence of living your life without Him.

If a person doesn't want anything to do with God, there is an eternal place reserved for those where there is nothing to do with God.

A person who stands at this sinners' judgement called "The Great White Throne" is a judgement of the Father Himself when a person is found outside of their body and yet still standing outside of the Blood of Christ. The person in this condition, cannot be judged by the Blood of God's redeeming Son, but upon the consequences and fruit of the sinner's own action or inaction. The only question that will matter outside of your body of flesh is: **"what did you do with and concerning my Son Jesus."**

Every person who finds themselves standing at THIS JUDGEMENT SEAT OF CHRIST is eternally damned.

These ones are eternally damned to a place called **the lake of fire.** This is the Greek word geenna. In every case this Greek word occurs it is actually uttered by the Lord Himself in the 4 gospels. This is a place of eternal torment, as opposed to eternal destruction.

There is a popular false teaching in the church called "annialism" or annialationism" that falsely says that the Lake of Fire is where everything goes to be once and for all - obliterated from existence.

Even back to the last chapter of Isaiah we read that even after the creation of the new Heaven and Earth, this place called The Lake of Fire will stand as a warning forever for all to see. Hell is not a place of destruction, but a place where you are forever consumed but never completely destroyed – while still wide awake.

"And they shall go forth and look upon the corpses of the men who have transgressed against Me. For their worm does not die, and their fire is not quenched. They shall be an abhorrence to all flesh."

Isaiah 66:24 (NKJV)

This actually teaches, in context that one day there will be a "new Heaven and a new Earth" and the torment of the damned will forever stand as testimony to "both the goodness and severity of God."

The scriptures clearly teach levels of accountability resulting in torment and eternal payment for sin. On the bright side, the scriptures promise great reward, recognition and blessings "IN CHRIST" for all who are found faithful.

It is also possible to enter Heaven eternally but with NO REWARD. Let's read here about the believer's judgement:

The Judgment Seat of Christ

Therefore we make it our aim, whether present or absent, to be well pleasing to Him.

For we must all appear before the judgment seat of Christ, that each one may receive the things done in the body, according to what he has done, whether good or bad.

Knowing, therefore, the terror of the Lord, we persuade men; *but we are well known to God, and I also trust are well known in your consciences.*

2 Corinthians 5:9-11 (NKJV)

This judgement seat is a small, raised platform like you would use to reward an athlete or other competitor for their accomplishments. Here is the Greek word:

bema - a step, pace, the space which a foot

covers, a foot-breath, a raised place mounted by steps, a platform, tribune of the official seat of a judge. This is the place of authority where Christ does not "Lord it over us" but recognizes our love and patient enduring faith in Him and rewards each one accordingly - or not.

Now of this very same judgement seat, the apostle Paul also writes in another place:

*Now if anyone builds on this foundation with gold, silver, precious stones, wood, hay, straw, each one's work will become clear; for the Day will declare it, **because it will be revealed by fire; and the fire will test each one's work, of what sort it is.***

The "Judgement Seat of Christ" is where God's, eternal, Holy and pure fire from the altar touches the substance of the works in Christ that you set before Him.

If the Holy Fire reveals gold, silver and precious stones in the offering of your life, then your reward will follow through to the eternal realms forever as testimony to your love, intimacy and commitment to Christ Himself. You are rewarded there in Heaven for serving your Lord in the right way, by doing what was asked of you personally as a member of His Body in this earth before you die.

If anyone's work which he has built on it endures, he will receive a reward. If anyone's work is burned, he will suffer loss; but he himself will be saved, yet so as through fire.

1 Corinthians 3:12-15 (NKJV)

So here we see that the fire from the Holy Altar may also reveal that a person can potentially spend a lifetime "serving God" only to reveal the truth of the work that was supposedly committed and submitted to Him but was not worthy of Him. The Bible says that this type of person will still be saved, but with the smell of smoke still on his clothing, a thoughtful and sobering proposition if there ever was one. Let's read on…

Do you not know that **you are the temple of God and that the Spirit of God dwells in you?** *If anyone defiles the temple of God, God will destroy him.* **For the temple of God is holy, which temple you are.**

1 Cor. 3:16-17 (NKJV)

In Christ, you do not just commit to Him, but actually and totally **BELONG TO HIM.** You and I as believers, are actually His personal property.

The Bible actually refers to each of us as "his special treasure." You have value to the one who MADE YOU.

This shouldn't surprise you as we took that very nature from our God in that most of us who are parents, love our own children enough to die for them.

ACTIVATION:

Let's commit ourselves to Him wholeheartedly:

Please say these words out loud with me...

Father in Heaven, thank you for sending Jesus as my free gift of salvation by His Body and His Blood, once and for all for all of my sin forever.

I submit to Christ's broken body as my own.

I submit to Christ's shed Blood as full payment for all my transgressions.

I ask you to help me to serve everyday in a manner that is both worthy of You and pleasing to You, in Jesus' Name, Amen.

THOUGHTS AND QUESTIONS:

_____

You are who you are - at this moment because of what you have allowed yourself to think, over and over. Your everyday thoughts are an ongoing dress rehearsal for who you are going to be tomorrow.

David James

Chapter 6 -
Where do I go from here?

Your Life does not belong to you at all – BUT YOUR LIFE IS GOD'S – for Him to use and minister with you and through you AS HE SEES FIT.

WHO you are and WHAT you are is built and designed by your God in Christ, for His pleasure and purpose.

Just as Christ was fully and completely submitted to His Father in Heaven, so you must submit yourself completely to your Father in Heaven also, but by the Blood and Body of Jesus Christ so that you will be accepted by your God, and then able to serve your Master in whatever way that He requires of you.

I highly recommend that every person read, study and become VERY FAMILIAR with the entirety of John 14-17, the entire chapters. This is some of the most dynamic and practical understanding found in the whole of God's written Word. John in his gospel wrote:

<u>1</u> "I am the true vine, and My Father is the vinedresser. <u>2</u> Every branch in Me that does not bear fruit He takes away; and every branch that bears fruit He prunes, that it may bear more fruit. <u>3</u> You are already clean because of the word which I have spoken to you.

Abide in Me, and I in you. **<u>As the branch cannot bear fruit of itself, unless it abides in the vine, neither can you, unless you abide in Me.</u>**

"I am the vine; you are the branches. He who abides in Me, and I in him, bears much fruit; **<u>for without Me you can do nothing.</u>**

Notice here, that you are NOT EXPECTED to do anything WITHOUT HIM. He clearly says you cannot bear good fruit or do anything of value in His Eyes unless you are doing it with Him, In Him and For Him.

<u>If anyone does not abide in Me,</u> *he is cast out as a branch and is withered; and they* *gather them and **throw them into the fire, and they are burned.***

If you abide in Me, and My words abide in you, you will ask what you desire, and it shall be done for you. By this My Father is glorified, that you bear much fruit; so you will be My disciples.

John 15:1-8 (NKJV)

According to verse 7, you are ONLY a "disciple of Christ" — WHEN and IF you "abide in Him" and "His Words abide in you."

In other words: Read, study and strive to understand what is written in YOUR Bibles and you will glorify God in your life by bearing Godly fruit and truly be His disciples.

Being pleasing to God is easy when you stop trying to please Him **and realize Christ is "already pleased with you"** — because you chose Him over the world, the flesh and the devil.

Bearing fruit in this context also relates to your eternal reward at the judgement seat of Christ.

How can anyone know and benefit from the fact that you are a fruit-producing branch "in Christ" unless you are obviously bearing the sweet fruit found only in His Vine.

If a person can see, even from a distance, brown, scaly skin on your apples and fruit with unmistakable evidence of worms in them, will he want to eat one?

For me to live is Christ [His life in me], and to die is gain [the gain of the glory of eternity].

Philippians 1:21 (AMPC)

Paul the apostle saw his own life as completely and totally expendable for and towards the cause of Christ - as God sees fit.

We should see nothing in our life of any value unless it is circled and embedded in the cause and purposes of Jesus our Lord and Saviour.

And see, now I go bound in the spirit to Jerusalem, not knowing the things that will happen to me there, except that the Holy Spirit testifies in every city, saying that chains and tribulations await me. **_But none of these things move me; nor do I count my life dear to myself,_** *so that I may finish my race with joy, and the ministry which I received from the Lord Jesus, to testify to the gospel of the grace of God.*

Acts 20:22-24 (NKJV)

Again, we see in verse 24, although Paul KNEW imprisonment and severe trials were in front of him, he simply did not care, as long as he was able to preach the gospel. In spite of the threats and the chains Paul was not swayed by them in any way from the course His Lord had set before him.

What is of value to you in your life right now?

It is both a scientific and spiritual fact that your very life will move toward your most dominant thoughts.

You are WHO you are at this moment because of what you have allowed yourself to THINK, over and over.

Your everyday thoughts are an ongoing dress rehearsal for WHO YOU ARE going to be tomorrow.

Your life, the good and the bad today, IS THE SUM-TOTAL of everything you have allowed yourself to think and dwell upon yesterday.

This plainness of speech is illustrated no better than John 14:7 above which we just looked at...***If you abide in Me, and My words abide in you,*** *you will ask what you desire, and it shall be done for you.*

His Words on you and IN YOU will make you a mature and fully developed man or woman in

Christ just as He originally intended when He first "thought about you and wrote about you:"

*Your eyes saw my unformed substance, and **in Your book all the days [of my life] were written before ever they took shape,** when as yet there was none of them.*

Psalms 139:16 (AMPC)

Your God wrote a book that contains all your life designed in Christ BEFORE YOU WERE YOU.

God's Word in you, has the power IN AND OF ITSELF to transform you into a person that will reflect and enhance GOD'S IMAGE AND LIKENESS to the world instead of manifesting the old fallen and distorted image of sin. The old man – before Christ – was the dark manifestation of a life that could not hide from or live in sin any longer, because you saw the Lord!

You may be saying: "I can't help what I think!" That is simply because you have not taken the proper time and discipline to train your life to be conformed to His image instead of your own.

Please know "what you THINK about HOW think that God's universe should run" is worthless. I've actually heard people say things like: "it should be this way" or I think he should do this." – Never taking the time to research what HE actually said about IT.

Arrogance and pride have cost untold multitudes of sinners their eternity, when they could have had Christ and our Father in Heaven if they had only opened the minds and hearts to see the truth that had always been staring them in the face.

WE NEED GOD every day, and we need to do everything we can to have Him in us and with us!

Simon Peter, a bondservant and apostle of Jesus Christ, to those who have obtained like precious faith with us by the righteousness of our God and Savior Jesus Christ:

Notice here that even before Peter called himself an apostle, he called himself a **bondservant.** That is an old-timey word to most of us. Here is what that means: ***doulos*** - a slave, bondman, a man of servile condition. In other words, Peter "made himself a slave to Christ's will and dominion."

Grace and peace be multiplied to you in the knowledge of God and of Jesus our Lord, **as His divine power has given to us all things that pertain to life and godliness,** *through the knowledge of Him who called us by glory and virtue,*

by which have been given to us **exceedingly great and precious promises,** *that through these you may be partakers of the divine nature, having escaped the corruption that is in the world through lust.*

2 Peter 1:1-4 (NKJV)

Peter prays for a multiplication of grace and peace, in that order. When you are walking in His grace, you are walking in His peace. There are few things in our daily lives that are of more value than living "torment free." Then in verse 3 above, HIS DIVINE POWER "has given to us ALL THINGS that pertain to life and Godliness."

In verse 4, that "divine power" has also been given to us EXCEEDING GREAT AND PRECIOUS PROMISES that through these (great and precious promises) we may be able to "escape by flight from the moral decay" that is all through this fallen world outside of Christ. Now here's the best part: "that we might be "partakers of HIS DIVINE NATURE." Rest on that and meditate.

As a result of this, **_He has given you magnificent promises that are beyond all price, so that through the power of these tremendous promises you can experience partnership with the divine nature,_** *by which you have escaped the corrupt desires that are of the world.*

2 Peter 1:4 (TPT)

You need to come to the place where you can see and experience partnership with God's Nature. This is not a promise of Heaven that is to come later, but a provision for the "here and now present age of corruption and destruction" that we see every day on every side.

When you have God's Word in you and speaking through you, you are agreeing with WHAT HE SAID, remember, this is the same failure that started in the Garden of Eden in the beginning. Failure to agree with what God said - and IS SAYING - is the same as spiritual treason. This is why we MUST HAVE JESUS living and abiding in each of us. Living for God is not easy – it is impossible, which is why we have to have someone to take our place between us and our sin.

For in Christ Jesus you are all **sons of God** through faith.

Jesus is **THE SON OF GOD** but each of us by faith IN HIM AND THROUGH HIM are also **"sons of God."**

For as many [of you] were baptized into Christ [into a spiritual union and communion with Christ, the Anointed One, the Messiah] **have put on** *(clothed yourselves with)* **Christ.**

When you deliberately chose to join yourself in spiritual oneness with your Anointed Saviour, **you've clothed yourself - with HIMSELF.**

There is [now no distinction] neither Jew nor Greek, there is neither slave nor free, there is not male and female **for you are all one in Christ Jesus.** *And if you belong to Christ [are in Him Who is Abraham's Seed], then you are Abraham's offspring and [spiritual] heirs according to promise.*

Gal. 3:26-29 (AMPC)

We have been "MADE HEIRS" of God because of Jesus. What Jesus has received; we have the privilege to walk in ourselves. Do you realize that Jesus said that we would one day "JUDGE ANGELS.?!"

We need to discover WHO and What it is that our God has made us to be. As believers in our Lord Jesus Christ, no matter our gender or race, we are all one in HIM, and because we are in Him, we are Abraham's spiritual offspring benefiting from all of His promises just as if we were Abraham's natural children.

ACTIVATION:

Say this out loud together with me please:

My Father in Heaven. I am so grateful that you have made me a part of your family. It is as if you had always planned it this way, because in fact, you did.

Lord, you designed me to serve you, not because I am a servant or a slave, but because you want me to partner with You in your plans and purposes.

You want me to a partaker of your divine nature because you have made me your child.

I am here because of Jesus. I am here because He gave His everything for me, so I can join in with your eternal plans, in Jesus' Name, Amen.

THOUGHTS AND QUESTIONS:

Your relationship with your God will not flourish by taking a week or two off, any more than your marriage relationship will flourish by acting married one week and single the next.

David James

Chapter 7 -

Letting the Life of God flow through you…

Today we are going to dive into three of the most important things you should do all of the time in order to maintain and grow into an obedient and fruitful child of God.

Coming to Jesus is like setting foot over the threshold of a grocery store when you are hungry. You've made it to the right destination - but what do you do - now that you are standing in front of so many aisles and choices?

When you stand at the inner entrance of a large grocery store, it is important that you have enough focus going inside, to know what's good for you and what's not.

You need to learn to read food and ingredient labels so you can learn the difference between real food that your body will benefit from, versus "something you can eat" that will at least fill you temporarily.

Walking into a new life in Christ is very similar in so many ways to this trip to the grocery store. Let's look at the most important of these principles.

CONNECT to a Good Local Church or Fellowship:

There are a lot of choices of places that call themselves church, but how many of you realize that there is also a very real difference between a whole food, organic grocery store and a monster retail chain that caters to every product and person simply because it sells and for no other reason than that it sells? …

Likewise, just because something is parked in a garage doesn't make it a car any more than parking in a chair or pew on Sunday makes you or anyone else who is there a true, Godly believer.

In previous chapters we have talked about "fruit-bearing." Every believer who is true to their master in private will display good fruit in public.

When we see obvious contradictions in the life of someone who calls himself or identifies as a believer, but behaves in ways that seem to contradict that, we should have strong questions about their salvation and their character.

"Beware of false prophets, who come to you in sheep's clothing, but inwardly they are ravenous wolves.
Matthew 7:15 (NKJV)

The person described in verse 15 is not necessarily a false "**prophet**" but someone who is false in their heart in some way toward the Lord they claim to speak for and serve. This person could be a member of a home group, bible study, worship team or any other ministry on the pulpit or otherwise in the church in any way. They "look like sheep" but underneath, they are something else entirely.

When I was young, we watched TV cartoons. Everyone's favourite was "The Bugs Bunny Road Runner Show." One of these characters was "Wile. E. Coyote" who, depending on the plot, was always trying to get past a sheepdog that watched over a flock of sheep grazing down in a field. The trick was that the coyote would go back to his den and sew a full-body costume of a sheep from head to toe. When he put it on, he was seemingly able to sneak past the sheepdog with a bundle of sheep in his arms safely back to his den. The sheepdog then revealed himself as a sheepdog inside sheep clothing himself and of course Wile E. Coyote paid the price – again.

One of the main lessons of this little story isn't just that wolves in sheep clothing look like the rest of the Christians, but that one of the ways to spot them is that they often have sheep in their mouths, ready to tear and consume them.

This is obviously a large topic on its own, but one of the best tips I can offer is that all believers must become practiced at the art of fruit inspection. This does not mean that you attack or otherwise put down or shun those in the church that are just honestly growing into their spiritual shoes and makes some mistakes, but that if someone sets themselves up or is setup as a leader in a congregation and consistently displays "bad fruit," these people are to be discerned, avoided or dealt with in some measurable way – depending on the circumstance. At the very least, if they "look like a problem" they just might be.

*Now also we beseech you, brethren, **get to know those who labor among you [recognize them for what they are,** acknowledge and appreciate and respect them all]—your leaders who are over you in the Lord and those who warn and kindly reprove and exhort you.*

1 Thessalonians 5:12 (AMPC)

This makes the local church of very high value when proper discernment is exercised between true brothers and sisters in the Lord. Now back to the wolves and the fruit:

***You will know them by their fruits.** Do men gather grapes from thornbushes or figs from* *thistles? Even so, every good tree bears good fruit, but a bad tree bears bad fruit. A good tree cannot bear bad fruit, nor can a bad tree bear good fruit. Every tree that does not bear good fruit is cut down and thrown into the fire.*

Therefore by their fruits you will know them.

Matthew 7:16-20 (NKJV)

Godly acts of service and fellowship toward the unsaved and fellow believers are needed and valuable and are usually good indicators of the maturity, content, and character of people in general. Every person who has come to Christ should find a way to go to a church or other similar place regularly where believers gather.

The body of Christ as a whole is made up of individual parts growing up into our God just as your little toe on your right foot is connected to the top of your head in some way.

Knowing your God "for yourself."

We recently read in John 14:1-7 that we, as individual branches are to be vitally and substantially connected to the Vine, our Lord Jesus.

Now, what you have been reading and hearing and watching as you've followed through with me in these lessons is the result of some person other than you who took the time and effort to draw close to the Lord so you could also come close to the Lord yourself.

You cannot be intimate with your God and the Lord Jesus by His Spirit vicariously through me or any teacher or minister any more than you can be intimate with your spouse while someone else is having sexual relations with them on your behalf.

The steps you take to draw close to your God on a day-to-day basis are to be determined, deliberate, and most of all consistent.

Your relationship with your God will not flourish by taking a week or two off, any more than your marriage relationship will flourish by acting married one week and single the next.

READ, Study and Learn to Practice Obeying the Scriptures:

Consistent attention to the scriptures, that is, reading, study and meditation of God's Word in its entirety as it is written in the Bible is number 2 on our list of the 3 main, purposeful things you must do to remain in close fellowship with the One who saved you and gave Himself for you and to you in the first place.

*But he who looks carefully into the faultless law, the [law] of liberty, and is faithful to it and perseveres in looking into it, **being not a heedless listener who forgets but an active doer** [who obeys], he shall be blessed in his doing (his life of obedience).*

James 1:25 (AMPC)

So Jesus said to those Jews who had believed in Him, **If you abide in My word [hold fast to My teachings and live in accordance with them], you are truly My disciples.** *And you will know the Truth, and the Truth will set you free.*

John 8:31-32 (AMPC)

Notice that it is only the "truth that you KNOW" that can benefit you in any way and in James 1:25 - it is only the *"active doer"* of God's Word who will walk in God's blessings in a vital and consistent way.

This again makes the local congregation so important as it gives us all many opportunities as we meet and gather around our Saviour to watch over each other in love if we hold ourselves accountable to each other IN LOVE preferring one another.

LEARNING to Hear God's Voice.

Most believers would love to hear and know from their God, by His Holy Spirit in them, what He is saying and thinking about them and their family and loved ones.

The Bible itself, that is: "the study and memory or scripture" is the ideal landing strip for God's clear and unadulterated voice in and around your life.

His voice in you by His Spirit - the very presence of God in you - is your lifeline to your Lord as to how He leads and ministers to you and through you - ALL OF THE TIME. God's voice, no matter how it sounds, will ALWAYS CONFIRM and not confuse or question the Word of God that you have come to know and understand. If you hear something you can't seem to understand or agree with that is going on in you and around you, the Bible says to "ask Him for wisdom about it" and the inspired spirit IN YOU will invariably lead you to 2 or 3 passages of scripture to either confirm or deny a thing.

Sometimes, a thing may be true, but you simply don't know enough. This is where the congregation can really benefit as others may be more discerning or knowledgeable about an area of God, His Word or a work of the Spirit for which you lack knowledge of.

All of these things taken together are built-in "checks and balances" that are designed to keep all of us, all together on the narrow path laid out before us. Those that are mature are supposed to nurture and disciple those who want to go deeper in God but also need strength and support in their weaknesses at the same time.

Now you [collectively] are Christ's body *and [individually] you are members of it, each part severally and distinct [each with his own place and function].*

1 Corinthians 12:27 (AMPC)

You don't need to specifically KNOW your exact part or "ministry," that is, you don't have to put a label on it to obey God's commands RIGHT NOW!

You don't need to be able to say: "I am this or that _____, ministry – just to fill in the blank.

We each know enough to DO something for our God. Even if all you know is your testimony, you still know what God did for you.

You are not required to know and explain your Christianity at all times to all people, but you know enough to be able to tell anybody what your Lord Jesus means to you and has done for you. The most important means to consistent, fruitful living is actually being a witness in all that you say and do.

But in your hearts set Christ apart as holy [and acknowledge Him] as Lord. **_Always be ready to give a logical defense_** *to anyone who asks you to account for the hope that is in you but do it courteously and respectfully.*

1 Pet. 3:15 (AMPC)

Last, but definitely not least is - through all you do in your walk with Jesus, make sure Bible reading and study of His Word is always thorough and consistent for every day of your life.

The "landing strip" for God's Voice in you is His written Word firmly planted inside you.

Our God honours you when you honour what He said. You will fall deeper in love with your Lord as you go deeper in His Word.

ACTIVATION:

My Lord God, in the Name of Jesus I take my place as a son in your house. You said I should "come boldly to the throne of grace, that I might obtain mercy and find grace to help in my time of need.

I belong with You. I'm part of You and You are part of me.

I ask you for a clear heart and mind that understands your Word so I can be obedient to DO IT, in Jesus' Name, Amen.

THOUGHTS AND QUESTIONS:

It has become popular today to say "my pronouns are _____" whatever you woke up and felt like you were. Notice there in John 14 that the Holy Spirit's pronouns are <u>HE</u> and <u>HIM</u>.

David James

Chapter 8 - The Holy Spirit

The Holy Spirit is perhaps the most misunderstood member of the Godhead.

All too often He is referred to as a "by the way" or just in passing so He can be properly ignored day to day in our lives. We are out to change that in your life right now...

This portion could easily have been placed much earlier in this teaching, but I have decided to put it toward the end, so that we will all remember that none of the earlier chapters in this message would even be possible if not for the continuing, abiding work of the Holy Spirit who is living in each and every believer by our Lord Jesus Christ.

None of what you have read, seen or heard in these lessons would even have been possible without the direct and substantial work of the Holy Spirit on the inside of me to teach it and even on you – in order to receive it and put it to action.

*Abide in Me, and I in you. As the branch cannot bear fruit of itself, unless it abides in the vine, neither can you, **unless you abide in Me.** "I am the vine; you are the branches. He who abides in Me, and I in him, bears much fruit; **for without Me you can do nothing.***

John 15:4-5 (NKJV)

We are revisiting this verse because it is so critical to not miss this. I did extensive research on that word "nothing" and discovered what it really means is NOTHING - that is - a big fat "0" with the rim knocked off...

*Therefore, it is said, When He ascended on high, He led captivity captive [He led a train of vanquished foes] and **He bestowed gifts on men.***

Ephesians 4:8 (AMPC)

What I or any other believer does in this world by the way of ministry of any sort is only possible as a result of the deposit and endowment of spiritual gifts our God has given each one of us. I am a multi-talented person. I am very good at a lot of things – but THAT is not necessarily ME at the core of what God truly values. The Spirit of God releases the direct manifestation of the deposit of His Nature into my life that is both from my mother's womb and subsequently, from the womb of the Spirit of God who drew me to the cross and saved and secured my future and my complete inheritance in Christ.

Any way you examine it, I am not the author of any of my gifts or talents by any definition. I am the author of this book, and very thankfully, but I can tell you of a certainty, without His anointing in me and upon me, NONE OF IT is possible!

YOU - have a divine deposit on the inside. Your inner man is made up of a spirit and a soul.

If you are a Believer, **<u>with your spirit - you are physically hosting the Holy Spirit in you.</u>**

With your soul, that is, your mind, will and emotions, you are hosting thoughts and ideas from a thousand separate places all at once.

All have experienced a moment when we might have been at work or school trying to solve a crisis or a math problem – while at the same time as you are doing that, you could just think of or smell chocolate chip cookies or something else that causes you to reminisce and you can be magically carried off to that special place and time in your mind - and that, only off of a smell.

Your life will, in the end, always gravitate toward your most dominant thoughts and memories. The work of the Holy Spirit in us is so multifaceted that it is impossible to function effectively as a believer and produce good, Godly fruit – without Him, so let's not even attempt to do anything without Him.

*"If you love Me, keep My commandments. And I will pray the Father, and **He** will give you another Helper, that **He** may abide with you forever—the Spirit of truth, whom the world cannot receive, because it neither*

*sees **Him** nor knows **Him**; but you know **Him**, for **He** dwells with you and will be in you.*

John 14:15-17 (NKJV)

Notice that the Holy Spirit is not an IT. An "it" is never referred to as HE or HIM. He and Him is mentioned 6 times in that short string of words.

If you love Jesus – obey Him.

The world can't receive Him. If you receive Jesus, you can receive HIM – The Holy Spirit. The Holy Spirit both dwells "with you" and "in you!"

It has become popular today to say "my pronouns are _____" whatever you woke up and felt like you were. Notice there in John 14 that the Holy Spirit's pronouns are **HE** and **HIM.**

I'm not just trying to be amusing, because much of the "modern church world today" has relegated the third person of the Trinity to the backseat driver that you would like to avoid or ignore so as not to listen to His directions.

The Holy Spirit is a person just as much as JESUS is a PERSON. Every member of the "trinity" has a specific purpose and manner of ministry.

The "job of the Holy Spirit" is to GLORIFY JESUS. In fact, one of the primary ways that you can help to discern whether a thing may be right or wrong, or good or bad, is to ask yourself, "does THAT glorify Jesus?"

*"But when the **Helper** comes, whom I shall send to you from the Father, the Spirit of truth who proceeds from the Father, **He will testify of Me.***

John 15:26 (NKJV)

That word "helper" is this word ***"parakletos"*** - it means intercessor, consoler, advocate, comforter - one who pleads another's cause before a judge, a pleader, counsel for defense, legal assistant, an advocate.

I NEED HELP every single moment of every day and The Holy Spirit is always available.

When Jesus was on the earth you would have had to get in line or wait for an available or otherwise appropriate moment to speak or counsel with Him. Now that the Father sent the Spirit of His Son into our hearts, we have complete and unfettered access to our Father God and the Lord Jesus Christ in all their fullness.

Now please understand that "Christ" is not Jesus' last name. This word is a title describing WHO HE IS because HE IS anointed by and with the Holy Spirit. **"Christ"** literally means **anointed.** The gift of the Holy Spirit was given to Jesus because of WHO and WHAT God made Him. Jesus then turns it all around and sees to it that you and I, and all who come to the Father IN JESUS' NAME might receive the "gift of the Holy Spirit" - again because of WHO and WHAT our God "has made us IN CHRIST."

In so many words, YOU are useful to God "in Christ" because the Holy Spirit anoints YOU. It is also a fact that God did not publicly use Jesus until HE also, was anointed by the Holy Spirit.

*"I still have many things to say **to you**, but you cannot bear them now. However, when **He**, the Spirit of truth, has come, **He** will guide **you** into all truth; for **He** will not speak on His own authority, but whatever **He** hears **He** will speak; and **He** will tell **you** things to come. **He** will glorify Me, for **He** will take of what is Mine and declare it to **you.** All things that the Father has are Mine. **Therefore, I said that He will take of Mine and declare it to you.***

John 16:12-15 (NKJV)

Of all the scriptures that talk about the work of the Holy Spirit today, for me, those 4 verses in chapter 16 might be the most fun and challenging. Also notice that HE or HIS occurs 10 times – HE doesn't sound like an IT does HE?

HE will guide YOU **into all truth.**

HE will speak to you WHATEVER HE is hearing from the Father TO YOU!

HE will tell YOU **things to come.** The Spirit of God knows the future and He will share it with YOU!

Everything that belongs to the Father belongs to Jesus, then **everything that belongs to Jesus is declared over and shown to YOU** when YOU are "in Christ."

Look at all the **YOU** attached to the promised Holy Spirit. He sent the Holy Spirit FOR YOU! If that doesn't thrill you, perhaps you aren't paying attention. Your God is not in the habit of hiding things "from you" – He revels in hiding things **"for you."** Your God asks YOU to seek Him.

The blessings and continuing favour of God do not simply fall on you like ripe cherries from a tree, they must be sought out, discovered and deliberately activated in your life.

*"Ask, and it will be given to you; **seek**, and you will find; **knock**, and it will be **opened** to you. For everyone who asks **receives**, and he who **seeks finds**, and to him who **knocks** it will be **opened**.*
Matthew 7:7-8 (NKJV)

Seek – Knock – Receive – Find – Open

Yes, our God can and does many things for you and in you and others without directly asking permission, but your ongoing relationship with your God, by His Spirit in you, is where the bulk of your spiritual life will be lived day to day for the rest of your life.

Our God is both calling and drawing up "deeper" into Him. The number one way he accomplishes this is by ministering in, to and through us by The Holy Spirit.

It should go without saying that volumes could be taught on the "work of the Holy Spirit," but most importantly we must GIVE PLACE and **MAKE ROOM for HIM to move in and through us every day of our lives.**

ACTIVATION:

My Father. I ask and receive the Spirit of Truth to lead and guide me INTO ALL TRUTH.

Help me to glorify my God every day, more and more - as I learn to yield and obey His promptings, feelings and directions.

I submit to your Word Lord.

I submit to your Voice Lord.

I submit to your Spirit in me right now so that I will one day hear my Lord say: "well done, good and faithful servant, enter into the Joy of
your Lord."

All of these good things in my life are by YOU, for YOU and because of YOU in Jesus' Name, Amen.

THOUGHTS AND QUESTIONS:

_____

I will flat out testify that no one thing I have done since my initial salvation has had more effect upon my family, business, life and ministry than speaking in other tongues through the spirit in me.

David James

Chapter 9 - The Holy Spirit and His Gifts

It is critical that you understand and appreciate that there is a very real and biblical experience we call the "baptism of, or in the Holy Spirit." We will be talking about that in this final chapter.

As we are about to read. A group of people in Ephesus believed the preaching of John the Baptist speaking of the ONE who was to come and follow him. When these disciples heard "there was more" they very eagerly and wholeheartedly" accepted Jesus, got water baptized, and then received this next experience when the Holy Spirit came upon them...

WHILE APOLLOS was in Corinth, Paul went through the upper inland districts and came down to Ephesus. There he found some disciples.
And he asked them, ***Did you receive the***

Holy Spirit when you believed** [on Jesus as the Christ]? And they said, **No, we have not even heard that there is a Holy Spirit.

And he asked, Into what [baptism] then were you baptized? They said, Into John's baptism.

And Paul said, John baptized with the baptism of repentance, continually telling the people that they should believe in the One Who was to come after him, that is, in Jesus [having a conviction full of joyful trust that He is Christ, the Messiah, and being obedient to Him]. On hearing this they were baptized [again, this time] in the name of the Lord Jesus.

And as Paul laid his hands upon them, the Holy Spirit came on them; and they spoke in [foreign, unknown] tongues (languages) and prophesied.

Acts 19:1-6 (AMPC)

Notice the question: Did you receive the Holy Spirit at the time that you received Jesus?

These were just "average people in Ephesus."

With no prior instruction, the first thing they did was "speak in unknown tongues and prophesy." I came to saving faith in Jesus in October of 1980. Only a few weeks later I found out from a Christian friend in my building that there was this other thing – an experience he called the baptism or being filled with the Holy Spirit. I was a very hungry and excited new believer at only 20 years of age. When I heard that, I said in myself "I must have that – I will get that. If there is more, I want it!"

In early 1981, in a large hotel ballroom on the southside of Edmonton Alberta Canada I received this baptism of the Holy Spirit at a Full Gospel Businessmen's meeting. I went forward to receive at the altar. Someone prayed with me. I instantly received and I immediately went to my car in the parking lot where I sat there and prayed in tongues (in the spirit) for about 3 solid hours.

Unfortunately, few things have been as attacked and vilified as this pure, holy and dynamic experience from my God. That tells me, when it comes to satan and the enemies of our faith, this must be very important to our spiritual growth and maintenance.

Know that we are talking about tongues and targeting this amazing Gift of the Holy Spirit in this last chapter, **because it is THE KEY to the best application of all of the gifts** as well as possibly the most important exercise of your faith you can do that will make you stronger and keep you in faith.

I will flat out testify that no one thing I have done since my initial salvation has had more effect upon my family, business, life and ministry than speaking in other tongues through the spirit in me.

Tongues Defined:

Tongues is the particular language that my spirit uses to speak to my God in a way and pray over things in a way that would not otherwise be possible.

When I don't know how or what to pray for a person or a situation, the Holy Spirit unction in my spirit allows me to release words and prayers that are outside of my mind and thoughts. I can allow it to flow for minutes or hours **because this form of "personal prayer tongues" is at my discretion and control.**

In effect, the words and language of each person's (speech) tongues will be determined by who they are, along with their maturity in the things of the spirit and a few other things. Now the language of the spirit is but one tool in a list of 9 specific manifestations of the Holy Spirit through the individual believer…

There are diversities of gifts, but the same Spirit. There are differences of ministries, but the same Lord. And there are diversities of activities, but it is the same God who works all in all. ***But the manifestation of the Spirit is given to each one for the profit of all:*** *for to one is given the word of wisdom through the Spirit, to another the word of knowledge through the same Spirit, to another faith by the same Spirit, to another*

gifts of healings by the same Spirit, to another the working of miracles, to another prophecy, to another discerning of spirits, to another different kinds of tongues, to another the interpretation of tongues. ***But one and the same Spirit works all these things, distributing to each one individually as He wills.***
1 Cor. 12:4-11 (NKJV)

It is not my purpose to do a complete and comprehensive teaching on this important topic, but to open the door for you to receive all that our Lord has for you as you grow up into Him.

As long as we are in this flesh body and not in Heaven, we will need tongues and all of the gifts in full operation. Since "tongues" are a stumbling block to many in religious culture and in many religious and liturgical churches, I will mention that there are different "tongues" in scripture, with different applications and different purposes.

On the Day of Pentecost, as recorded in Acts chapter 2 (you should get familiar with at least Acts 2-4) tongues in this initial manifestation were a SIGN to all of the foreigners gathered at Jerusalem for the Holy Feast, as the 120 in the upper room spoke in languages that were understood by the visitors to the city.

Another manifestation on tongues taught by Paul the Apostle is in 1 Corinthians 14 is where Paul speaks to the difference between tongues as a public manifestation (with interpretation) versus the speaking in tongues that was for the individual believer in their personal and private time that is for the edification of all believers for their spiritual growth and edification individually.

There is much to say on this topic, and I will be eventually dedicating a full series of messages to the Holy Spirit and His Gifts, but for now I will say that **wherever we see it mentioned throughout the Book of Acts, the baptism of the Spirit or infilling is ALWAYS accompanied by tongues,** except in only one verse where it is obvious and inferred though not specifically mentioned. What is most practical for you to know is that to receive anything from God you must have an open heart to receive and never assume something is wrong or even spiritually demonic, without careful examination and study.

Be aware that Jesus warned the Pharisees and religious leaders of His day sternly that ONE SIN COULD NEVER BE FORGIVEN...

*Wherefore I say unto you, all manner of sin and blasphemy shall be forgiven unto men: **but the blasphemy against the Holy Ghost shall not be forgiven unto men.***

*And whosoever speaketh a word against the Son of man, it shall be forgiven him: but whosoever speaketh against the Holy Ghost, **it shall not be forgiven** him, **neither in this world, neither in the world** to come.*

Matthew 12:31-32 (KJV)

In the full context of this scripture, Jesus warned that **when a person says some work of the Holy Spirit is actually a demon** - this cannot be forgiven.

Understand that these religious leaders were held to a high level of accountability because of their knowledge. It doesn't mean if you've ever misunderstood tongues or otherwise mocked a work of the Holy Spirit, that you are eternally damned. I strongly encourage all who read and hear these lessons to be open to God and His Holy Spirit in you. You don't need to be afraid of a wrong spirit or a devil when you come to your Lord asking for HIM…

And I say unto you, Ask, and it shall be given you; seek, and ye shall find; knock, and it shall be opened unto you. **For everyone that asketh receiveth; and he that seeketh findeth; and to him that knocketh it shall be opened.** *If a son shall ask bread of any of you that is a father, will he give him a stone? or if he ask a fish, will he for a fish give him a serpent? Or if he shall ask an egg, will he offer him a scorpion? If ye then, being evil, know how to give good gifts unto your children:* **how much more shall your heavenly Father give the Holy Spirit to them that ask Him?**

Luke 11:9-13 (KJV)

God's Kingdom way is always voice activated. You confess Jesus as Lord, and you will be saved. If you don't deny Him, He will not deny you.

Be sure to pray the Holy Spirit activation at the end of this book - **after you have for certain, confirmed Jesus as your Lord and Redeemer…**

In my experienced opinion, tongues for the personal edification of the believer - is perhaps the most satisfying spiritual exercise you can ever participate in.

I KNOW that my God has sustained me, preserved me and moved me and others forward in ways I can only imagine now through my prayer language of tongues. Only in Heaven will I learn what was accomplished from the use of my prayer language.

*But you, beloved, **build yourselves up [founded] on your most holy faith [make progress, rise like an edifice higher and higher], praying in the Holy Spirit;** Guard and keep yourselves in the love of God; expect and patiently wait for the mercy of our Lord Jesus Christ (the Messiah)—[which will bring you] unto life eternal.*

Jude 1:20-21 (AMPC)

I can tell you for certain that my walk with the Holy Spirit IN ME is the most important thing I can concentrate on and there is no more practical way to do that than the exercise of the "personal Gift of Tongues" in the believer.

*If ye love me, keep my commandments. And I will pray the Father, and he shall give you another Comforter, that he may abide with you for ever; Even the Spirit of truth; **whom the world cannot receive,** because it seeth him not, neither knoweth him: but ye know him; **for he dwelleth with you and shall be***

in you. I will not leave you comfortless: I will come to you. John 14:15-18 (KJV)

Jesus was preparing His disciples for the soon reality that He would no longer be with them, but that also that they would not be left orphans.

Also understand that the Holy Spirit can only be received by a BELIEVER.

The Holy Spirit from the Father comes to those who have FIRST RECEIVED the Spirit of His Son into their hearts and lives. As a believer in your Lord and Saviour Jesus, you were never meant to do this life down here without Him. Quite the opposite. Remember the earlier lessons...

*I am the vine, ye are the branches: He that abideth in me, and I in him, the same bringeth forth much fruit: for **without me ye can do nothing.***
John 15:5 (KJV)

We have prayed much throughout these lessons, but I want you to be SURE that Heaven will be your Home and Jesus will be your Lord and Saviour through eternity outside of your body. Remember, nothing else matters UNTIL IT DOES MATTER, and then you will be ready and you will not be afraid.

RECEIVE JESUS AS LORD, SAVIOUR and REDEEMER OVER YOUR LIFE:

Father, you said in your Word that if we come to you in faith, we would not be rejected or cast out.

Romans 10:9-10 says that "if we confess with our mouth and believe in our heart the Lord Jesus we shall be saved."

God, I come to you in the Name of Jesus and ask for your cleansing blood and forgiveness eternally over my life now.

Jesus, I call you My Lord, Saviour and Redeemer NOW.

I am a believer. I am Saved. I belong to you, in Jesus' Name, Amen.

HOLY SPIRIT ACTIVATION FOR BELIEVERS:
Father, I ask you to baptize me in the Holy Spirit NOW, in Jesus Name.

You said, "ask and you shall receive, that your joy may be full."

I ask that the fulness of the Holy Spirit manifest in me NOW.

I open my mouth by faith boldly and I will speak by the spirit in me, and you will give me the words.

Remember, IT IS YOUR SPIRIT SPEAKING TO GOD, not God speaking to Himself – does that make sense?

Now open your mouth, move your tongue and your lips and form and release the words that are rising up out of your own belly!...

When you begin this activation, you will feel a stirring inside you that is hard to explain. This is the unction of the Holy Spirit in you, inspiring the words that **"your new, redeemed spirit wants to speak to your Father**.

This now becomes a most vital part of your ongoing communion and fellowship with your Father, who isn't just in Heaven, but actually abiding in you with HIS SPIRIT.

Congratulations, now never stop speaking in tongues. Use it everyday and in every way to build yourself up and talk to your Lord in ways that are not possible without it.

Remember, according to 1 Corinthians 12, all of the Gifts of the Spirit are there for your benefit in some way. Some of the gifts will flow though you for others, while some of the gifts will flow though others for your benefit.

I will see you in Book 2 coming soon:

PRACTICAL FOUNDATIONS FOR THE VICTORIOUS BELIEVER

Landing on the Higher Levels

THOUGHTS AND QUESTIONS:

_____

ABOUT THE AUTHOR

I came to saving faith in Jesus at 20 ½ years of age in October 1980. Early on in my discovery, I immediately became desperately hungry for all there was that I knew God wanted me to have and experience.

My first most desperate desire was to receive the baptism of the Holy Spirit as a new believer in Christ. Just a few weeks later I was speaking in tongues, a heavenly prayer language available to all who ask and receive.

Within the first 3 or 4 years I knew that I was called as an Ephesians 4 teacher to the Body of Christ. Since then, on my road to eternity, I have taught in prisons, from the pulpit, in Sunday school, website articles and finally my YouTube channel, which, as of this writing has grown right up to near 50,000 subscribers in about 7 months.

Under the Lord's direction, this is Book 1 of a 3volume set designed to practically help every believer to grow up in God.

I reside in Kelowna BC Canada where I am still married to my first wife, have 3 grown children and 1 grandchild.

In my other life, since 1993, I have been the owner operator of a thriving construction renovation business.

For more information and other materials please visit me at:

thrivingintheendtimes.org

There you will find a wealth of free articles, as well as links to all of my videos and teachings.

Be sure to visit my **YouTube** and **Rumble** channels and subscribe at:

Thriving in the End Times with David James.

Join me also on **X** and **Truth Social**

If you have questions or comments - email at:

thrivingintheendtimes@proton.me